Also by Maureen N. McLane

MORE ANON

MAUREEN N. McLANE

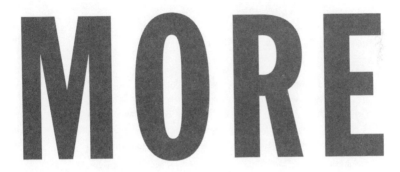

MORE

SELECTED POEMS

ANON

FARRAR, STRAUS AND GIROUX
NEW YORK

Farrar, Straus and Giroux
120 Broadway, New York 10271

Printed in the United States of America
First edition, 2021

Library of Congress Cataloging-in-Publication Data
Names: McLane, Maureen N., author.
Title: More anon : selected poems / Maureen N. McLane.
Description: First edition. | New York : Farrar, Straus and Giroux, 2021. | Includes index.
Identifiers: LCCN 2021006861 | ISBN 9780374601980 (hardcover)
Subjects: LCGFT: Poetry.
Classification: LCC PS3613.C5687 M67 2021 | DDC 811/.6—dc23
LC record available at https://lccn.loc.gov/2021006861

Designed by Crisis

Our books may be purchased in bulk for promotional,
educational, or business use. Please contact your local
bookseller or the Macmillan Corporate and Premium Sales
Department at 1-800-221-7945, extension 5442, or by
email at MacmillanSpecialMarkets@macmillan.com.

www.fsgbooks.com
www.twitter.com/fsgbooks
www.facebook.com/fsgbooks

10 9 8 7 6 5 4 3 2 1

Life is, generally speaking, a blessing independent of a future state.

T. R. MALTHUS, *An Essay on the Principle of Population*

Spare us from loveliness.

H.D., "Orchard"

Experience is a hoax.

ALICE NOTLEY, "Experience"

*

I see thee in thick clouds and darkness on America's shore.

WILLIAM BLAKE, *America: A Prophecy*

Contents

FROM

MZ N: THE SERIAL: A POEM-IN-EPISODES

(2016)

FROM

SOME SAY

(2017)

MORE ANON

envoi

Go litel myn book
and blow her head off

make her retch and weep
        and ache in the gut

make her regret everything about her life
        that doesn't include me

SAME LIFE

were fragments enough . . .

were fragments enough
for a life

for a fiction
of continuity

in our every cell
a tiny alphabet restricts itself

to the possible
mutations,

evolution
proceeding along lines

imperceptible
as the day

I was thrown
from the imaginary car

& broke the barrier
of this carrying life

it is true I take pleasure
annihilating all the world

to a penned thought caught
in a fan's whirring blade

Catechism

Did your mother like you
      She was afraid of me

And the kindergarten
      Glowed like the yellow sno-cone

And the dingding man
      Was gentle kind & true

How old are you
      This is my last incarnation

Where did you first see the morning glory
      Sometime before the millennium but long after I had grown up

What foods
      Chicken pizza powdered milk

What foods
      Vegetable biryani flautas falafel asparagus turbot

And then
      I fell in love three times each time was violent and small things
      smashed and bloomed

What world
 The place I live is only sometimes shareable thus weeping

And after
 That day I realized calm that something tremendous had
  happened to me but I had not noticed

Diagramming sentences
 For a long time I used to go to bed early

Finally a beginning
 There is one day it will all end for me

after sappho IV

it's true the charm may lie
                    somewhat
    in the subject such as gardens
                            wedding songs love affairs
against these few will speak and all
                            at one time
        may have hoped—
but there is your bending
            neck and the small hollow at the base
                of your long back
        and no charm
            other

    song likes its own delights and even sadness
            in some modes
                        charms
                            those whose hearts have moved
                so

            what to do with the soul
                        its many
                            motions

after sappho V

and you
whom I will likely never see again
I hope it has all gone well
    that the lover has finally left his wife
    that roses now climb the trellis you'd staked
    and you've left the less-than-stellar job—
      —perhaps everything is changed

you deserved every gift
    you never got and all the ones
      you did. you led so many
      onward and if when they arrived
        they found themselves
          alone, aflame—

      you above all know I was left
      so, my insides ash—

      why blame the fire
      for its damage?
      for so long it gave a lovely light—

and when I last saw you
    and you so lightly said

o wait there love   *o wait a moment love*
how could that bird
    in my throat
        tho I had snuffed that all out
            not revive

Terrible things are happening . . .

Terrible things are happening
                    in Russian novels!

        Just yesterday I heard
                        in the café

                    of two peasants, long friends,

                    one in sudden possession
                                    of a watch
                                            hanging
                                            from a gold chain

            which so disturbed his compadre
                                    he stole
                    upon the other unsuspecting, prayed
                                    to god

                    and slit his throat, fleeing
                                        with the watch—
                            and that's not the worst of it!

Just yesterday my love and I too
                    had not exactly a "fight"

but a "reckoning"

        perhaps, or no—a

               "conversation" which opened the ocean

               of grief

and now she is in another city

        perhaps crying

               and not because of Russian novels

Excursion Susan Sontag

Now Susan Sontag was famous
among certain people—you know
who I mean—urban informed culturally
literate East Coast people and some West
a few in Chicago in Europe and elsewhere although
Susan Sontag came from Arizona
which is remarkable
only if you hold certain prejudices
about Arizona which I do
having been there twice
and disliking it both times
not that this was Arizona's fault
it is majestic strange lunar orange desert
flat and then ravine-ridden but Phoenix
is heinous unless you have a certain
po-mo sensibility I associate with men
of a certain age and race and while
I share the supposed race I'm not a man although
there are men in Arizona but I forgot
to ask them what they thought
about the state or Susan Sontag
whose writings between 1964 and '67
are marvels of incisive thought and style
so much so that you have to wonder

what happened to America
what happened to Susan Sontag
who later published historical novels
in a realist mode when earlier she
championed the *nouveau roman*
oh where art thou where art thou Robbe-Grillet
and did her execution fail
her once-held prose ideals
oh is it our fate thus to lapse
if lapse it was and where is Sontag
to show us how to read Sontag
a professorial enthusiast
ringingly declared one Sunday Susan
"is always of the moment"
and thus we must conclude that in 1965
the new novel and criticism and sexy brains and France
were of the moment and now degraded realism
is of the moment as is "ethnic cleansing"
which Susan Sontag denounced indeed "put her life
on the line" (viz. enthusiast) producing Beckett
in Sarajevo she among the few
who spoke truly after 9/11 while torpor
overtook so many everyone waiting
for American Special Forces to "smoke"
Osama bin Laden "out of his hole"
on this matter Susan Sontag
held strong views e.g. about the president's
speech but she properly oriented us
to the club of men and one woman who advised him

since as she observed in an interview
on salon.com we are living in "a regency"
and we all know that regents are puppets
of their wily advisers cf. The Prince Regent
in England 1819 when aggrieved workers
gathered in Manchester and cavalry
trampled them tens dead hundreds injured
the papers covering up the massacre
whither media complicity is history now
and in England the people I met read several papers
expecting to compare and contrast each paper's
"take" on the news they didn't simply succumb
to the infantile American fantasy of media
"objectivity" the English and Irish
and Scots were like Burke unafraid
of prejudice they understood
you read through/with/against others'
prejudices and your own and thus Burke
against himself may be seen as an Enlightenment
theorist he supported the American Revolution
after all though he hysterically denounced
the French long before they guillotined anyone
o sweet Marie your fair chopped head
your luscious body the French pornographers
delighted in fucking tormenting reviling there
is a long affair between Enlightenment
philosophy and pornography as Cathleen Schine
explored in her spiky novel *Rameau's Niece*
as Sontag explored in a brilliant essay
of 1967 why are we so afraid

of porn there are many reasons the obvious
Freudian ones the "porn is rape" ones
the "protecting our children" ones the fear
of desire for the tabooed the "jouissance
of transgression" the world could blow up
any time but at the end
of the day it may all come down
to this our desire for knowledge
rips open the throat whole countries
have been seized with murder when threatened
with free inquiry not that those
who affiliate themselves self-righteously
with knowledge are not guilty of their own
simplifications because knowledge cuts
and opens wounds and distances
between lovers parents children citizens the world
feels different for example if you know
that somewhere people think god is dead
if the earth revolves around the sun
if you have stolen the gift of fire
if you know where your clitoris is and what
it can do and if you've seen Mapplethorpe's
whip stuck up his ass or his little devil's horns
perkily perched atop his mop of hair
why does he look so innocently rakish
is it because he's dead or that moment is or
is it my own perspective makes him so
not everything can be domesticated
or can it why did Proust avoid discussing
really discussing the mother now there is a crucial

evasion in an otherwise exhaustive
registration of the movements of consciousness
in society must old rockers and ACT UP veterans
and the Situationist International and Sontag all go
gentle into no that good that no that raging

From *Mz N: the serial*

Like all children Mz N lived
in archaic
mythic zones
and all the neighbors and kin played their parts to a T
although they never were able to tell her
the whole story.

*

The child Mz N sat on her bed
and wondered: that tree
outside her window
shifted
when her eye
shifted. What to make
of that?

*

Mz N and her siblings
had a dog for some time.
They went on vacation &
when they came back
no dog.
They asked the parents:

the dog?
who replied:
what dog?
And some people wonder
why others distrust the obvious.

     *

One year Mz N began her great project
of investigative
touch. Like everything
it came about
through reading
and happenstance. Mz N had a friend
who said I do it and then
I worry
what if my roommate
hears?
What if?
Mz N wondered
went home
and discovered a new octave.

     *

Mz N sometimes thinks
what N stands for: Nothing.
One day she said
nīhilism
in school & the teacher

paused, chalk between her fingers
like her longed-for cigarette.
What's nīhilism
another student said I thought
it was *neehilism*.
This was another example
of Mz N bringing up topics
that went Nowhere.

*

the blackest black
is not so black
it cannot take
a blacker black

so Mz N thinks
the void would speak
if void could speak
or of color think

*

Mz N is writing what she hopes will be
a masterpiece: *Mispronunciation:*
the definitive
autobiography. She only includes
the bloopers she remembers.
She is very strict like that.
What's vá-gi-na

—hard *g*—
she called to her parents
age five
when they'd plopped her on the sofa
with a picture book
to help her learn
where babies. Some years later she told a story
at dinner
about being very angry
with a persecuting
teacher. I spoke
she sd
with great ve-**hé**-mence.
Her father laughed
a somewhat unkind laugh
and asked her to repeat it.
She did & once again
he laughed.
Mz N vehemently
objects to the making fun of children
who struggle every day
to get their words
and bodies aligned

    *

one day after sex
in a century of bad sex
the other one asked Mz N
did I leave you

on the edge
never having had an orgasm
as far as she knew
she sd
quite definitively
no
how would she know
such an edge
are you sure
the other persisted
Mz N thought again
she could say
quite definitively
oh yes here I am on the edge
where you left me
the edge
of a certain
abyss
but this
she knew was the answer
to a question
no one was asking

*

Mz N embarks one day upon a sonnet
attracted by the knowledge that it's dead
extinct like dinosaur dodo or bonnet
long replaced by baseball caps on heads

that centuries ago were piled with curls
birds powder wires and such machinery
'twould blow the minds of tattooed boys and girls
who cruise the streets of this new century

Mz N concedes she's antiquarian
old hat old news—"hoarder of ancient dirt"
to quote the mouldy Scot John Pinkerton
but from her dead-end path she won't divert

the airplane made the train a living fossil
relict herself she listens for its whistle

*

Wordsworth never took a plane
but Mz N takes a plane with Wordsworth
on her mind
and other matters: love,
fear, a wish
to die.
Wordsworth had a very sturdy mind
and legs that took him far
into the mountains,
Scottish glens, German
towns and yes across
the Alps. Mz N has never seen
the Alps nor Snowdon
nor a mountain
anywhere beyond the ancient

Adirondacks Wordsworth too she thinks
would like their worndown humps
their pathless woods the rowboats by the shores
of placid lakes ready
for exploring. Young Wordsworth stole
a rowboat
rowed out on a lake one night and found himself
appalled
the mountain strode sublime
after him
and he trembled and his mind
as Burke had said it would
before sublimity
near failed. There are passages
in life
in Wordsworth
he called spots
of time and Mz N has some spots
she sometimes
recollects. But now
she's happy incredulous
in love
and in strange anguish
wants to recollect
nothing. *If it were now*
to die
'twere now to be most happy
she murmurs
with the engine
nearly exploding

with the fragility
and perverse strength of all that lives
and moves and has its being
in the air on the ground in the sea.
Having reached a floating state
of grace, surprised
by joy
she wants to die
life
can only get worse
the mountain
receding below them as they climb

Letter from Paris

The French are universal
    particularly in their regard
        for their darker brothers

who under the majesty of the law
    are prohibited equally
        with the white and the rich
    from sleeping under the bridges of Paris.

    The heavy shining stones of the 3rd Republic
and the iron filigree of a thousand balconies
        sing struck by the wind
    & a broom beating a carpet
& the children shout in the playgrounds
    their voices in school
        so ruthlessly suppressed—

The American chain stores have landed
    despite *patrimoine*
    but foie gras persists
        untroubled by the protests
        of Californians
—& surrounded by so much self-evident
        finishing off
    it's hard to resist

the trimmed leather jacket
the furcoat that floats by
             as natural as the clouds
& the roast innards of a
             million beasts gone
       to a long acculturated death.
If I am out of joint
       it is because I have gone
             completely allegorical
& my old dreams
       of wholeheartedeness
& a justified life
       have flown out the window
like yesterday's suicide
             off the Montparnasse Tower.

             It is best to avoid
       grotesque similes but someday
             these likenings
       may become precise
as the watches the Huguenots perfected
       before they fled
to the Pays-Bas and South Africa
       & elsewhere
carrying with them a sober intricate knowledge
             of weaving and timepieces
             & the Hebrew Bible.
I am drawing up an indictment
       of the French
       & Reason

& Human Rights
which begins by unlinking these concepts
    and concludes in weeping.

    Revolution is not only disappointed love Antoine.
There was a time when the earth and every common scene
        featured a green clearing
        where men and women
            grew strong in their sweet regarding
    each other as fellows and their children
        newsprung in a
        new world—

We have written this story again
        and again
and that it was written
        does not make it false
whatever the logic of pastoral
    and its oblique compensations
        for "the real" we never "experience"
        —its impossible promise
            of a shepherded life—

    the thing was that shining—

    let us not put a date
on what now seems forever to be disappearing—

Poem

As a man may go to Costco,
Buy the jumbo pak of diapers, double liters of
Coke and Diet Coke and a sixpack and stock up on
Doritos and Cheetos and
Eveready batteries, so I perhaps
Formless in the vast republic
Grasp the metaphysical thing, commodity, crucially desired
Hologram of national intent. Caught
In the managed aisle the
Jargon of experts washes o'er the perfectly stacked Special
K, Cheerios, Wheaties, Apple Jacks, and Count Chocula
Low on the shelves that toddlers might harry their
Mothers for sweet breakfast treats. In
Niger the children and livestock go hungry
Once more but a fortified peanut butter paste
Plump'ynut promises to revive those babies
Quickly who are not yet too far gone.
Research has given us hope that *all*
Shall be well and all manner of thing shall be well
Till the moment it's not. It's not.
Unto the lord Julian of Norwich poured forth her
Voice. Into the desert the Tuareg
Wander, their herds and children starved. Between ocean
Expanses a people of plenty chatter brawl and sometimes
Yawn. Days so short it seems the earth is
Zooming unto its longsought anonymous abyss.

regional

birches by the tracks
beyond them the pines as we rattle by
haven after haven west and new snaking our way
to the first city of the republic
of which the historian of the american south remarked
"if I could live my life in any era
I would choose boston circa 1820"
inspiring diverse thoughts among the students
listening or not as they pleased because pleasure
will make its crooked steel-tied way to the heart
of the assembled population
even in new england

Core Samples

When I met you I was eighteen
bitter as the bolted lettuce
neglected in the garden.
Your laugh had a hiss.

You lay in the bathtub
choosing between me and her,
both of us singers.
For some reason she would not sleep with you.

That was long ago.
You have a young daughter,
another wife.
I am sure you never tell her

how it was with us.
You were always discreet.
Now I sit by roses
not missing you and your long silences.

*

Those were the years I fell in love
with every woman I knew.
All my close friends touched my tongue
at least once, then returned to their sensible husbands.

Sometimes we arrange to meet
and after some wine they remember
and blush and wonder
and ask if I too wonder.

It seemed one could be anyone
those liquid nights.
I now walk by a river with my lover
and they go to their several homes
carefully shutting the doors.

*

It was under the spell of Yeats I fell
in love with you, though it may have gone back
to Chaucer. One night I had a dream
I was a heroine in Spenser

and woke up burnt, branded
by your imagined touch.
There came a day in spring
when stung by your faithless lover

you were more than ready for another.
That day we read no further.

You wanted to be seduced.
At that time I could not play master.
Your breathing got faster
as you leaned, desperate, into your desired disaster.

*

You I never fell in love with.
I confess it was an experiment
and perhaps unfair. In my defense
let it be said I experimented more

on me than you, who were already beholden
to your "erotics of surprise."
I did not wish to be surprised.
With you I saw how far I could go

away from myself. On the open ocean
the sun beats hard and true
and your thirst is never relieved
except by what you bring with you.

You gave me to know this
and gave me an illness
you didn't even know
you had. They tell me
you're never wholly cured.

*

I never made you breakfast.
Thank you for the coffee and the toast,
the encouragement to get the piano
—but let's forget the rest.

It was never about lust
you sd, thrilled to be so honest
and casual by the lake.
I thought you were a fake.

I was sick of your music
and sick of the sex
that was rarely more than anemic,
a studied thrust & suck.

Still it amazes me
after that talk
and the lake turning black
you thought I'd come back.

    *

Sad in bed you read Horace
the ode in which an aging lover pleads
not to be inflamed again
by a perishable love

and a tear escapes his eye
and a tear escaped your eye.
I was wild for you and heedless
I am glad love to say this

I was afflicted and afflicted you.
Be careful what you wish for
you warned. I was not careful
nor in the end thank god were you.

The charms I recited
the songs I sang
were lit by a light
almost wholly impersonal.

Yet what are we but vehicles
of waves we never directly perceive
except those days the light bending
around our bodies becomes our body
—the lovers ablaze on the pyre

syntax

and if
I were to say

I love you and
I do love you

and I say it
now and again

and again
would you say

parataxis
would you see

the world revolves
anew

its axis
you

I wanted to crawl inside . . .

I wanted to crawl inside a middle voice
of a Tallis motet and sleep

the centuries away but the promise
of a cadence lured me awake

in the woods the air aflutter
with alien birds seeking a branching grace.

there was a form for beseeching
and a form for praising

never too far from the anchor
never too far from the shore

and now a passing note
blows the body into another world

WORLD
ENOUGH

Passage I

little moth
I do not think you'll escape
this night

I do not think
you'll escape this night
little moth

*

bees in clover
summer half over
friends without lovers

*

I bite a carrot
horsefly bites me

*

I thought it was you
moving through the trees

but it was the trees

I thought it was your finger
grazing my knee

it was the breeze

I thought prayers were rising
to a god alive in my mind

they rose on the wind

I thought I had all the time
and world enough to discover what I should

when it was over

I thought I would always be young
though I knew the years passed

and knowing turned my hair gray

I thought it was a welcome
what I took for a sign—

the sun . . . the unsymboling sun . . .

*

watch the clouds
on any given day

even they don't keep their shape
for more than a minute

sociable shifters
bringing weather from elsewhere
until it's our weather
and we say now it's raining here

*

Vermont shore lit
by a fugitive sun
who doesn't believe
in a day's redemption

*

sunset renovation
at the expected hour
but the actual palette
still a surprise

*

gulls alit on the lake
little white splendors
looking to shit on the dock

*

little cat
kneading my chest
milkless breasts
take your pleasure
where you can

*

not that I was alive
but that we were

L.A.

Let me say first
    oleanders—oleanders and cactus abounded
    as if commandeered to grace a set
        idea of the place. And

        the pastel stucco'd rows
   and London planes lining the sidewalked
      avenues as if anyone walked
         or biked and England
           existed. These

        are stereotypes
     so let's sing them
      in stereo:

     I love L.A.   I love L.A.

and what is nature
but the about-to-be-
transformed or the never-
to-be or whatever
is & is & is and lacks
       a finishing touch—

The pools imply a plein air delinquency
the Hockney blue of this one
its kidney shape echoing
my two
as I've been taught by beans
and X-rays and forensic
anatomists

a gaggle of kids kibitzing
round a common table
the great American mashup visible
at the poolside bar

the children of the Pacific
the Sikh black-beturbaned
and perhaps scimitared
& other faces shining Spanish and indigene
announce a west so beautiful
and confabulated the idea
of the desert recedes

Saratoga August

rain rain and the trees
engulfed I am tired
of reading Russians their suffering
souls their tribulations
excavating a dank
depth they surely have a word for
that fatal Russian soul—
easy to see
how a blast of speed
called light might clear
the air the heavy hooves
of the horses now stopped
from racing a mile
away. Swaying
cedars, a light
wind and a low canopy
of clouds belie the summer
you recall from the calendar.
If I say spring
& you think September
you might be from Australia.
If I say love & you think sex
you are not Thomas Aquinas.
I am not worried
about my brain

today or TV or the latest war
in the Caucasus.
Creepy philosophers
isolatos in huts
articulate a theory
of care. I close
my eyes & the world
disappears.
You open yours
& the clouds rearrange
themselves shuffling
the birds.

                *

wow the latest hysteria
our version of a rain dance
o it's coming friends the endless
rains we longed for danced for
& the deserts
we thought we knew
will be thickly forested
in the blink of some creature's eye—

geography's back
& new maps and the dolphin's
displaced by sick tones—

how anyone thought music
            meaningless

or universal   how anyone thought
         thought alone
would have everything to do with it—
         the wind picks up
         a cloudshift's sense
         transferring whatever—
         the helplessly metaphorical wind—

         *

that wind rushing through the trees
         was the rain. That sun you saw
through a cracked windowpane withdrew
         for days but only
from us. The specific ticks of raindrops
         individuating
themselves against the eaves ledges roof
         & beyond; behind
the indistinct fuzz of a general
         rain. What you call fog
he calls a cloud. What you call rain
         is raining every day

         *

rising up from below
the insistent swell of a downpour
now annihilating the flurry of pings
of a rain just seconds ago
distinguishable
from air

*

have I become a
              meteorologist
of moods no clear
              taxonomy or predictive
power to move out of
              this loafing groove

*

If I say rain
almost straight
for 14 days
you'll get a picture
not inaccurate though the sun's allowed
an almost daily swim
for a core crew
of lapswimmers.
Too bad for the divers
the funsters cannonballers
disciplined into invisible lanes
though Chana for one often veers
and merges without signaling—
Yo Chana! Watch out!
The yogi devised eight steps
to a clean heart and body
mere abstention from sex
insufficient. From the general drift
of talk it seems no one

is chaste or aspiring.
Fuckbuddies
there may be
but no one's really
prying; that's how we know
it's a reasonably genial
crowd—the gossip's
anthropological.
         Some nights poker,
other nights screenings, *Scenes*
from a Marriage, George
Washington, though some are dying
for a mindless buddy movie
some kickass comedy to purge
the blood burdened
with high thoughts.
         There's a fetus here
by which I mean a pregnant
dame—a gal I used to know
when I was 17 and cringing
at the dormroom door—
return of the repressed
indeedy. Little fetus
for now dubbed Oslo
by one and all
needn't screen out nada
right now unless he's freaked
by the talk in the Lino Room—
they say it like *rhino, lino*
for linoleum a residual

Britishism ghosting
this place that's lost
a lot of that crap. Today
I stumbled on the graves
of the founders, benefactors
—it must have been nice
to be here those years
not so nice with Robert Lowell
et al. on a manic
Commie-hunting spree.
No Russians here but in town
some waitresses have that Slavic
tilt to their eyes & in CVS
I encountered a blonde
so perfected it was clear
she was imported arm-candy
for one of the bigfellas
at the racetrack. Many here
are divorced
or will be & this is emotionally
difficult and statistical
like life
in general. No one touches
on this in the idyll unless
it won't break the spell
to invoke it. The cold
war's long over and meanwhile
it's just us chickens
brooding and happy
not to think
about what's next.

*

if I say thunder
and you answer lightning
were you already so near
I could touch you
—and *thunder*
& you turn off
your computer—
were you listening
to me or the weather
report? I'm not getting
any younger
says the thunder
to the sky—
I'm not moving
any farther says
the cloud that won't pass by

*

what god
takes these pictures
paparazzo
to the universe
violent bulbs
each bolt
flashing the black
world violet

*

among several games
a choice few
are favored—Poker, Mafia,
the occasional bout
of Boggle. Here
It's All Primates
All The Time
but the question
remains: bonobo
or chimp?
Have you hooked up
with S? M asked L
in the pool. Score one
for M! Soon
the inspectors
will arrive to measure
the chlorine, announce
all is well
or not. Meanwhile
the lapswimmers
swim on dreams
of Olympians spurring
their imperfect strokes
—utopian dreams
don't come from nowhere.
It turns out
the pool
inspector works in the local

liquor store—and here
he is, a beer
for all and tucked
in his pocket the chemical
testing strips.

*

Three down with rumored
Lyme but antibiotics are saving
us all from the worst
for the moment. If I say
we charmed the sun
with spells of guava rum
and grapefruit punch you should believe
it was a swell pool party last night
this morning's benediction of eggs
sunny side up
proving it so. If not everyone came
well that's OK, we can feel it
waning, the days, the months,
the season, our casually shared
lives. Intimations
of immortality are all very well
if all shall be well
but intimations of nothing
are more useful
if you have a residual
Calvinist soul. You don't need
to be a voluptuary

of death or dream or your dark
heart to want to know how its shaping
hand is shaping every hour. Heedless,
heedful, what's needful
is what we sometimes ask
when surfacing from a freestyle
lap, the pool bottoming
the abyss. O reason
not the need but can one help but reason
when it seizes the works and days
of our thinking. You'd never know
who was good in bed, at poker, at pool
unless you put yourself
through it. The sea calls
for drowning, the pool
for floating, some days
for lounging. If I say
cypress and you think
mourning you might read Latin.
If I say hemlock
and you think trees
and Socrates you will not be surprised
by our priceless ignorance.
Let us devote a week to nothing
that will not give pleasure.
Let us devote a life
to what's not to like
in this world if what's not to like in this world
is moving us into
the next—

*

and finally
sun
in the morning
proving
morning
after all
the time
of sunrises

*

see you've already forgotten
      the rain
in the cumulus courting
      the sun
it won't block—forgotten
      the pull
of the moon just past full
      is affecting
the waves. The song
      of the cardinal
flaring the hemlock so long
      ago rang out
so long ago nothing belongs
      to that rain
gone so long you've almost
      forgotten
how long ago rained down
      the rain

Haunt

There are too many cedars here
            hiding the sun hovering
                        over the dead
            the lakes won't wash away
& the ghosts the locals talk of
                        are their memories
            singing and shifting unbidden *I heard it*
                        last night *I saw it*
                        on the staircase
            testimony weaving its own
                        shimmering cloth
            we wear to keep ourselves warm
                        & to spare the others
                                    our nakedness
            —better not to have heard
                                    the stories
                        the dead children
            lunatic mothers gimlet-
                        eyed servants and
            absentee lairds
the old murder ballads in Scotland
            depend on
there's a dead soldier on auld fail dyke
            on yonder greene plain
            a knight centuries ago

there's a dead woman in the river
dead baby in the cradle
      there's a dead soldier in the desert
& three crows wonder over and over
      whether to cry out
         an elegy
      or to sit on his breastbone and pike out
         his bonnie blue een

Songs of a Season II

Sun through the thick glass
Another morning come—
Dreams done dawn passed
Sun through the thick glass
A faint light, the day's cast.
What's done is done and done.
Sun through the thick glass,
Another morning. Come.

*

To want to be awake
Every hour, to miss nothing
Of the changeable air, the lake.
To want to be awake
In the light and starred dark—
Every instant another thing
To want. To be awake
Every hour. To miss nothing.

*

A tender mist barely there
In the morning. A soft sun,
Dew on the grass, light chill in the air—

A tender mist barely there.
August near over. What to make clear
Before the end of the season?
A tender mist. Barely there
In the morning: a soft sun.

*

The husband I never think of
Returns one night in a dream
Who were those people? The moon above
The husband I never think of
Shines its indifferent love
Shines its unwavering beam.
The husband I never think of
Returns one night in a dream.

*

sun in the cedars
the moon in the pines
the day breaks itself clear
(sun in the cedars)
of the moon in the pines
and everyone sees again how it ends
the sun in the cedars
the moon in the pines

*

Have I been resting
My elbows in birdshit?
Are there birds nesting
Above, flinging direct hits
Where I have been resting
My arms? Was it a blue tit
What done it? I have been resting
My elbows in birdshit!

*

Was it merely personal
This interest in one's own life?
Each morning brought the same birdcall.
Was it merely personal
The persistent cardinal?
He sang in the cedars, a red knife.
Was it merely personal
This interest in one's own life?

*

The grandparents sink
Below the horizon
Like their parents before. Unlinked
To the earth, the grandparents sink,
What they were what we are soon indistinct.
The effort of living done
The grandparents sink
Below the horizon.

*

Morning sun gone
Clouds in the hemlock
The wash undone
Morning sun gone
What should I have done—
Called the friend, taken a long walk?
Morning sun gone
Clouds in the hemlock.

*

"Good looks will only get you so far
And that far I fully intend
To go." So she says, smoking in the car—
Good looks will only get you so far.
Scanning for lines in the mirror
She considers what Botox won't mend.
Good looks will get you only so far
Whatever you fully intend.

*

No escape from the endless chatter
Of people on cellphones
Talking as if it all mattered.
No escape from the chatter,
The world to be nattered
Away in a blizzard of blank tones.

No escape from the endless chatter
Of people. Cellphones.

*

Time to admit
That misanthropy
Has a logic to it.
Time to admit
Some days you'd quit
The species and flee.
Time to admit
That misanthropy.

*

What happens in one place
Will soon happen everywhere
Wrote the man with the seamed face.
What happens in one place
Will not be confined to that place,
Will spread and soon displace
What happens. One place
Will soon become everywhere.

*

Do you still think of me
As I still think of you
When I'm by the sea—

Do you still think of me
When you pass that stand of cherry trees
That bar on 81st only we knew—
Do you still think of me
As I still think of you?

*

Never again to visit that place
And never to think of it.
Never to see again that face
Never to visit that place
Never to try to stash the suitcase
In an overhead bin it won't fit.
Never again to visit that place
And never to think of it.

*

The language bore me along.
Before I knew anything
There was its welcoming song—
The language bore me along.
Strange to have gotten so wrong
So much, to know nothing
But language that bore me along
Before I knew anything.

*

Who were you to her
And who was she to me?
At 3 a.m. I wonder:
Who were you to her
And what did you murmur
To her when you suddenly saw me?
Who you were to her?
And who she was to me?

*

Those little crushes
That sneak up
Tiny ambushes
These little crushes
Betrayed by flushes
You can't cover up
Those little crushes
They sneak up

*

Five weathers in one afternoon—
A day seemed a year seemed a life
Seemed a cloud become a balloon—
Five weathers in one afternoon.
However it changes the moon
Rings its changes each riff less brief
Than the weather this afternoon.
A day seemed a year seemed a life.

*

Three and then four fell—
Dull thuds in the heat
That made the fruit swell.
Three and then four fell,
Loosed by the wind, the reddening apples
The deer come at dusk to eat.
Three and then four fell,
Sweet thuds in the heat.

*

Your tongue in my mouth
In the afternoon light
Your breath in my breath
Your tongue in my mouth
Your breast on my breast
In the unbreaking heat
Your tongue in my mouth
In the afternoon light

*

Not yet burnt red
The maple's tip, no frost
To flare it so. Not yet put to bed
The roses, not yet burnt red
The mountain, nor yet bled
Dry the pipes. No trees lost

This season's storms, nor yet burnt red
The maple's tip. No frost.

*

And suddenly: Autumn,
The long endless sun over
And soon too the crickets' hum.
Thus suddenly: autumn
Misgivings—so little begun
So little recovered
When suddenly: autumn:
The long endless sun over.

Au Revoir

We did not go to Versailles.
The ocean did not turn over.
The moon remained unmanned
and two teams called out in turn Red Rover Red Rover.

Did Fisher-Price furnish our minds
with a transportable *imaginaire*?
George Bush the first said he liked pork rinds.
My name not Mary my self contrary.

Things are always terrible
for some people. The question
is the ratio of the palpable hurt
to the general session

of life in an era. Narcissism
the Hall of Mirrors multiplying
me and you and me no schism
between ourselves and our lying

ideals. This is another first-world poem
annoying in all its presumption
its feckless tourism presupposing a home
and its hubris misregarding itself as gumption.

Autobiography cannot anymore be spiritual
and the obviously sexual dimensions
of experience laid out before all
a spatchcocked chicken the cook mentioned

she'd make you for dinner
after she serviced the young monsieur
on the staircase. *It's hierarchy or chaos*
mister sd the structuralist seer

a woman no friend
to women but no enemy
either. How to end
the impasse. How to be

perfectly complicit to just the degree
you deserve asked the dominatrix
by which I mean post-structuralist
for whom the question of rubber vs. latex

moves us far beyond rational choice . . .

Anthropology

why am I not preserving
      the yanomami language
      or speakers of same
or learning a lusty romance tongue
      the smell of the sea
      mediterraneanizing open vocables
           split down the middle
           by dirt?
o the language game uh huh. I played
      the lion, saw that I won, sd
      hello. He like unto himself
           yawned/roared
           as the case required.
a daggered paw ripped off my face
      the savanna no longer so peaceful—

all this was caught by the cameras
      the intrepid documentarian brought
      in the jeep.

bleep bleep went the machine
      begging for love
      thought the anthropomorphizers
and right they were: desire slimed
      everything.
how stupid to forget the objects
      would one day rise up

Life Study

Just as I must draw
to see
the world eclipse
itself before
my oblivious eyes
as I must draw to register
the retinal
flash of reality
effects my brain insists
on generating
to help me live
"life"
"not working out
too terribly well but I think
I'll keep going"
optimism
ridiculous
not to honor
the upsurge
as the dog frisks in the street
and the students smoke & glower & parse
their way
into situations
they forget
in a decade

but the smoke haze
lingering in the old walls of the rue Suger
however often cleaned
life
a revenge
upon memory
I disbelieve
in continuous
ribbons of identity
yet who else
did that past
happen to
waylay
last night
in the dream
that had me
up against the remembered wall

Song of the Last Meeting

A few roses were blooming
on the almost bare trellis.
Your hair was now short.
I had never seen you that way.

All morning I'd wondered
whether to wear this
or that skirt.
It might have mattered.

It was strange to see you
in a new house
shining as you sat
in a necklace of raw flowers.

And when later in the café
you were so quick to flare
at any casual thing I said
I saw how you must have flashed
for all your lovers.

Songs of the South

lavender freighted
with bees

pursuing their task
pursuing their pleasure
bee labor or leisure—
conundrum in the lavender
lavender conundrum

white butterflies
in the lavender

and now a derelict red
butterfly amidst the lavender bestarred
with white

and now amidst the lavender
bestarred with white butterflies
a derelict red butterfly

to what end
the white moths now alighting
in the lavender

II

no bees could labor
to make sweeter
the honey
your thighs

III

for white say wheat
for blue blé

I will mow your hay
my love
before the end of day

IV

poppies scattered
ungathered—

oleander
meander

V

Get Drunk the poet sd
and we did

THIS BLUE

A Situation

Everything bending
elsewhere, summer
longer, winter mud &
the maples escaping
for norther zones . . .

Take it up Old Adam—
every day the world exists
to be named.

Here's a chair,
a table, grass.
A cricket hums
my Japanese name.

Skyscrapers
are stars. Rocks.
Those were swell,
seasons. So strange,
that heaven, that hell.

Aviary

Curmudgeon
pigeon,
iridescence
glinting unlike
granite,
what common
gullet did you peck
that crumb down now
you jerking thing
some call a flying
rat? Rats will inherit
the earth's garbage
dump and you
may also flash
on that trashheap
called the future
untransformed.
Yet to the dove
you're kin.
If my love
could sing
like a mourning
dove, could ring
the wrongs
away in the wind . . .

Kind bird,
do what's yours
to do with every
scrap forgot—
the nightingale's
not more precious
than your idiot
insistence to stick
around and peck and look.

Summer Beer with
Endangered Glacier

My one eye
does not match
the other

Corrective
lenses regulate
whatever

needs require.
Seeing?
I was being

being seen.
Let be
be finale.

Let our virtues
tally
up against

the obvious.
If we
don't believe

ourselves
custodial
why all

the hoobla-
hoo, hulla-
balloo?

Passivist
mon semblable
ma soeur

soi-même
blow through
this blue

All Good

a "beautiful day"
nothing happened
and nothing was going to happen
the wind shook leaves
that did not fall
the moored boat did not sail
& the rain fell
on casual grass
everything was full
including the empty glass

*

a "beautiful rose"
no sign of a woman
but a boy's succulent anus
in a Persian lyric
call it ranunculus
or camellia
are they not more enfolded
than the folded rose
whose folds your nose
now probes

*

the mountain's
promiscuous
any cloud can take him
any sun have him
it's all good
today's assent
and tomorrow's

What's the Matter

Why the low mood,
the picking at food?
Maybe it's the weather.

Maybe it's hormones.
Explanation's cheap
but sometimes hits the mark.

*I am the target
of mysterious arrows
I myself let sling.*

O that's your fantasy
of omnipotence.
You make everything
your thing.

All day I stayed in bed.
It seemed someone else
must have been alive

have done what I did.
Failed to do
what I failed to.

It's still in my head
those things I did
and said and cared for

doing but it's all gone
white like green hills
in certain light

as Dante says the hillsides
can go white
in the middle of a new life.

OK Fern

OK fern
I'm your apprentice
I can now tell you

apart from your
darker sister ferns
whose intricate ridges

overlay your more
regular triangled fans.
Tell me what to do

with my life.

Tell Us What Happened
After We Left

Ferns here ferns there
I dream of my newest friends
who will soon subside
into near strangers
—peculiar the sudden
intimacies evanesced
without a kiss . . .

Who went home
with whom after the dance
party's what we want
to know. What century
did seduction
end in? Libertines
linger in the corridors

of the purely sexual.
I pulled you up
by my bootstraps
& liked it. I licked
you up & down

& up. I poached
eggs on your breasts

and combed yr curls.
There was nothing
I wouldn't do
with you & to.

Let's go down
to the river none
returns from. O yes
you swift diver
you plunge good.

That Man

That man over there
looking sidelong
as you sidelong
smile I do not think

he's a god
or frankly that great
but it's true he's glowing
under your eyes &

obliterating
the sun that moments ago
was shining on this bench
where we sit across

from him now
flaring terrible
as I think of your
many rendezvous

I desire death &

I almost shove back
in my throat the call

to the Perseids calling them
down now to shower

him dead in their shower

They Were Not Kidding
in the Fourteenth Century

They were not kidding
when they said they were blinded
by a vision of love.

It was not just a manner
of speaking or feeling
though it's hard to say

how the dead
really felt harder
even than knowing the living.

You are so opaque
to me your brief moments
of apparent transparency

seem fraudulent windows
in a Brutalist structure
everyone admires.

The effort your life
requires exhausts me.
I am not kidding.

Genoa

The merchant republics are done
as is the nun
who forbade us aged five to say
we were done.
The oven door opened
in her mime
the door to the oven
where we were thoroughly roasted
and done.
If you are done
that means I can stick
a fork in you. You
she corrected
are finished.
Finished
with all that some days
it seems a dream
the long boredom
in the schoolroom
workbook assignments
rushed through straining
toward what weird
consummation?
Sister Lucretia—
she was another one
terrifying the children who braved

the zenana of nuns
pledged to Christ and torture
of the wayward souls who ventured
into the sanctum sanctorum
the private apartment of six nuns
for a weekly piano lesson.
Bach had twenty children
she declared. Her heart was given
to a Texan—Van Cliburn.
A wimpled nun
one of the last
thus to dress among the remaining Franciscan
sisters. Excess
daughters in immigrant families
ready to give some
aid and comfort to the Lord
or the local monsignor—
a special vocation—
were they rotting away
in their habits, were they
the transfigured ones?
I wanted once
to become one.
Those days are done
and I am almost done
almost historical as a usuried ship
heading west and more west
to find treasures
for kings. Look in thy heart
it is a treasury
it was said

Mary said.
She was another one.
Even now at the Brignole station
we see flocks of nuns
rope-belted, a crucifix flying in wind.
A veiled woman
might become another woman
under a different sun.
Even here the sisters
have become Indian, Ethiopian,
no extra Italian
daughters to pay the godly sum
of glorious renunciation.
The Turks are threatening Christendom
in old chronicles
and today's European bulletin.
Beware of falling under the thumb
of Islam.
It will never be finished
said the Caliph
to the Sultan.
It is almost done
this meal where I stick
a fork in tomatoed squid stew
called *buridda* its Arabic origins
brining my tongue.
I stick a fork in an animal
fork in a soul
and I eat and I eat
until kingdom come.

Ice People, Sun People

Something to it, the thought
of a people like its clime
or thereby impressed—
my lunchtime lassitude dissolved
the minute I moved from the sun
to this shadowed grass.

I could invent the wheel now
& soon the cotton gin
and steam engine &
let's not forget
it won't be long now
before nuclear fission.

Nothing's beyond
my airconditioned ken.
My offshore multinational's
humming more power
than the biggest powerstation in Hoboken.
My shadowed shade
my intemperate glade my big fat thrum.
Let's call it progress, this.
Let's call it whatever it is.

Terran Life

—AN EXCURSION BEGINNING WITH A LINE OF WILLIAM WORDSWORTH

When we had given our bodies to the wind
we found bones in the earth and not in the sky.
We found arrowheads in the earth and not in the sky though they'd flown
    through the air before grounding.
The era of common sense is over
& finished too the flourishing of horoscopes.
Hey traveler what chart to sign your way? what iPhone app?
All the birthdays have immolated themselves in a far pyre
and no one knows where
they were born.
Earth gods always come after sky gods.
If you could choose
a secret power would it be flight?—
a wish more often expressed
than the desire for invisibility.
"A mythology reflects its region"
and a poet sang the sea the lemon trees and pines
the Ligurian breeze salting his lines
and a lightly placed step on a Greek mountain is the goat song of tragedy.
Jehovah rarely shows his face for we would die of it
die as surely as those who looked to the sky in the bombing raid
the underground tunnels a sudden refuge

Out of ash I come   Out of the earth
Back to ash I go   He fashioned them
male and female I tell you
they wore the most beautiful evanescent clothes
in paradise so much subtler than the trawling nakedness of heaving giants
hurling other giants to heaven & some to hell
on the restored ceiling of the Sistine Chapel.

Thus far clones are of earth, alone.
When you say earth you mean land but more than land   You mean
    the oceans covering "the earth" as if earth were the substrate of
    everything and not also the crust.
I found the ground sound, unfaulted, uncracked, even where the
    continents have split and will again split the archaic seamstress
    unable to suture the plates of the earth forever.
"Terran life": what the biologists typically study but "weird life" is also
    a zone of research. "It is easy to conceive of chemical reactions that
    might support life involving noncarbon compounds"—
viz. *The Limits of Organic Life in Planetary Systems*, p. 6.

Earth now supports life but could not now initiate it.
Crawl, sway, sashay: you're still doing it on an earth
    you take for granted instead of going crazy
    yr head blown off by an apple no I meant an IED no
I meant an apple.
Newtonian physics' defunct but that doesn't mean an apple doesn't fall
    far from the tree composed of atoms whose dark matter you don't
    know how to measure, supermodel. Me neither.
Gravity thy name is woman

always secretly pulling me toward you
as if I had no resistance
as if the clothes I wore were merely draped
on a mannequin as if I were merely an earthbound species with new skin
that fur an old animal's fur
reclaimed by another.
Did you see the subtle shift from umber to somber to ochre on the walls of
    Les Caves de Lascaux?
What ibex steps as beautifully as you
what ancient bison shakes the steppes
what gazelle's ankles are so perfectly turned as yours?
There are no meth heads in prehistory but surely
we were addicted to something we hominids
strutting our way out of the savanna—

I demand the sun
shine on me
I demand the moon bare its face in the night
and lo! damn! see how these heavenly bodies do what they do
like clockwork before clocks
like skin before clothes
like the earth before the parting of the waters revealed
the earth was the earth is the earth . . .
And if she only likes vegetable things
that grow toward the light
and if she will not eat your roots and tubers
how then choose
between a rooting boar and an urban forager—
There is beauty in indistinct areas the microtonal

hover where the ear buzzes so—

There is a gasp a sharp breath in a sharp wind reminding

you the wind was someone's breath chilled.

Clouds are now fashionable as they were in John Constable's day Luke

    Howard having taxonomized the little buggers in 1803: cumulus,

    cirrus, etc.

So let's go skying with Constable let's scan

the horizon as if we were sailors

able to read the sky   Let's blast off

and outsoar the noctilucent clouds

I espy with my little stratospheric eye.

Do you think I'm afraid of crashing to earth?

Love we've been falling ever since falling made way for a leap.

Replay / Repeat

Amazing they still do it, kids—
climb trees they've eyed for years
in the park, their bicycles
braced against granite hewn
hauled & heaved into a miniature
New Hampshire Stonehenge . . .

Your white-pined mind
fringed with Frisbees saucering
the summer into a common
past—look, it's here! two red
discs! & the goldplated trophies
everyone gets for team effort.

Human beings always run
in groups. Sure there's a solitary
walker, can't bother
him, iPod breaking his brain
into convolutions
you'll never get the hang of.

Go skateboard yourself.
My maneuvers are old-
school, yes, but so's school

& summer & children
& these fuckedup resilient trees
which tell time like the Druids
by the same old same old sun.

Horoscope

Again the white blanket
icicles pierce.
The fierce teeth
of steel-framed snowshoes
bite the trail open.
Where the hardwoods stand
and rarely bend
the wind blows hard
an explosion of snow
like flour dusting
the baker in a shop
long since shuttered.
In this our post-shame century
we will reclaim
the old nouns
unembarrassed.
If it rains
we'll say oh
there's rain.
If she falls
out of love
with you you'll carry
your love on a gold plate
to the forest and bury it
in the Indian graveyard.

Pioneers do not
only despoil.
The sweet knees
of oxen have pressed
a path for me.
A lone chickadee
undaunted thing
sings in the snow.
Flakes appear
as if out of air
but surely they come
from somewhere
bearing what news
from the troposphere.
The sky's shifted
and Capricorns abandon
themselves to a Sagittarian
line. I like
this weird axis.
In 23,000 years
it will become again
the same sky
the Babylonians scanned.

Quiet Car

the willow's lost its hair
the snow's receded almost everywhere
and you are riding in the quiet car

the branches mostly bare
but the thin icesheets that cracked and chimed the pond
                    have vanished into water
while you are riding in the quiet car

walking around the reservoir
            canvasbacks gliding on the water
the path two miles, perhaps a bit more
while you are riding in the quiet car

soon I will climb in the old blue car
and drive to Back Bay, not too far
from you my love now riding in the quiet car

Enough with the Swan Song

The woods are words
the turkeys spell
with their feet
their pine-needled path
a wild way
we won't take.
The sheep that bleats
in the night escapes
a starry declivity
we must be rescued from.
The rocks rest
below mosses, the pines
outtop the hemlock.
Flat ferns fan the wind
that will not break
this heat. I am lonely
with the sculpted edges
of fat leaves on low shrubs.
Ingrate soloist the chorus
is just beginning
and that bodacious robin
doesn't care if you join.

MZ N: THE SERIAL: A POEM-IN-EPISODES

PROEM:
Mz N Contemporary

Mz N tries
each day very hard
to be contemporary
One must be
absolutely
contemporary
they've harangued
her for over
a hundred years
& who is she
to object?
She admires
after all
beyond Rimbaud
Yvonne Rainer
who in an interview
somewhere sd something like
I am so happy
to have been able to be
contemporary
or was it she was happy
to have made an art
wholly contemporary?
Well.

You're too young
to think so much
Yvonne sd
to Mz N
about death
Mz N felt oddly
abashed but what to do
You thought
whatever you thought
about. That's an evasion
the cognitive therapists
could flush out
of Mz N very swiftly
with their meta-mind techniques
and surely Zen Buddhists
and their American epigones would also say
let the thought pass through
just observe the thought as it passes
That was one
of many mistakes
Mz N kept making she held on
to a thought
as to the sharp end
of a knife
which puts her in mind
of an old Setswana proverb
Ellen Kuzwayo taught her
Mmangoana o tshwara thipa ka fa bogaleng
the child's mother grabs
the sharp end of the knife

but Mz N was not a good
enough mother to her thoughts
They raged and sliced
her barely surviving for years until
they didn't. A thought
isn't irrevocable
Arendt sd   Only action
Mz N would take action
against her thoughts
You think
too much her sister
sd which meant
why don't you
chill out?
Why
not?
Mz N
was no riot grrrl
there was no club
she could join to align
herself with weird sisters
or brothers. The three
punkish kids in high school
were heroes
in her private pantheon
but they like odd gods
were remote
as a loon calling
from a far Adirondack
lake. O there's a loon

on the lake I look at
right here right now
Now I am being contemporary
I can bring the now
right into this poem
& when I say
as I now do
with how sad steps
o moon thou climb'st the skies
I am still very contemporary
which is to say
I am alive
as long as this poem
I & the loon & the moon are alive

All the artists
Mz N knows
who are alive want to be
contemporary
It takes effort
to be contemporary
simply being alive
doesn't cut it
One artist made a piece
This is So Contemporary
which is elegant
and funny like him Tino
Sehgal a piece both contemporary
and a critique
of the enforcement of the law

of the soon-to-be-obsolete
now which consumer
culture and deep structural
forces of finance capital
sustain or so Mz N's been told
—O tempora O mores!
Dance and political economy
and game theory are intricate
choreographies of the now
Critique is dead
Poetry is dead
Tino told her
no one in Europe reads books
It is contemporary
to ironize the contemporary
but in a light way
no one bothers
anymore with the past
There is no longer an Oedipal
pathos or rage to fuel the now
sprung from the paternal then
Sometimes depth
is just depth
Brecht sd
to Benjamin when depth
was still an option
Mz N's deep
inwardness
is positively
German an unfashionable

Innerlichkeit
best cordoned off
in the foreign
dead field of lyric
Inwardness
an effect of repression
but hey
Don't fence me in!
the little dogie
of Mz N's soul
cried to the postmodern
cowboys lassoing
up the language
of reference & branding
it for sale
Sometimes Mz N even feels
conceptual
What is a concept
What is a conceptual artist
An artist
with a concept
Some days
one can't help being Horace
& writing
an ars poetica

All day
Mz N has been eating cherries
of a kind she first saw
in Cambridge 1989ish

when her friend Polly
with higher standards for fruit and men
and clothes went to the beautiful shop
on Huron Avenue and bought
these golden cherries
I now eat
as my memory is the fact
of my being alive
& her & you too
& the cherry ripe
I gave my love and that stone
I gave my love still ring
that song that cherry song
still ripe in our live mouths

Mz N Nothing

This is a tale
about nothing
Let's pretend
we have to establish
the scene & characters though movies
do it so much better
to the despair of the novelizing tribe
But let's say
the midafternoon sun
is striking the leaves in the woods
visible from a screened porch
such that the maples liquefy
into a queer green flame.
In the foreground
are ferns, a few daisies,
a black-eyed Susan
or two. Mz N regrets
what she drank
almost as much as what she said.
And then there's what
she didn't do—kiss
for example
the lithe lovely
in the purple sheath that hugged her ass
like the plumskin the plum.

She bites
the plum in her lunch
a lunch someone else
made. Further chapters
will unfold the full ecosystem
of labor and erotics
that structure the whole panoply
of exchanges
that make up "life"
which is the contract
I make with you reader
hungry as we are for the fruit
of the real

Mz N Triumph of Life

Some are alive
easy and slip
into the world's skin
as their own and plums'
Mz N isn't one
or wasn't
Then what is life?
I cried
cried Shelley
in one version
of *The Triumph of Life*
the title of which from one angle
is a satirical title
triumphs in those days
like Romans'
a chance to parade
the victims   in this case
the victims of life
which are in the end
from a mortal angle
everyone
Better never to have been
the old sage said
and each world
rediscovers

No river
No river twice
and yet it seems the same river
however
much you are not the same

He's not so bleak
that sleek and laughing
vegetarian poet

O could you not learn
to swim you idiot
singing yourself
aboard ships
you could sail
but not sail home

Just like you
to learn to sail
and not to swim

Just like Mz N
to dive in
after him

Mz N Highschool Boyfriend

There was a highschool
boyfriend there is always
one in young adult
novels since romance is outsourced
to the teens
as in Shakespeare
Mz N was no romantic
about this
very nice highschool boyfriend
she would have said
he was "very nice"
& the parents more or less
approved he seemed nice
undebauched sanitized etc
Mz N was vaguely
excited by the sex
thing which wasn't much happening
& this was irritating
but may have kept her just this side
of launching the chain reaction
& meltdown which would turn her soul
into Chernobyl
Mz N was a catastrophist
which was in her view
the highest realism

This is not the time
to retail the horrors
and pleasures of suburbia
so many
of both & you know them
from so many novels and movies
Mz N had never seen
It seemed overdetermined
to live in a town
named for a famous
lost civilization
Minoa was archaic
then & now the bull
moved his brute force
through her
dreams & she'd ride him
The boyfriend
was conspicuously
nice which was just what she wanted
& not. She was split
that way typical
split the good
daughter raging a beast
within. And so.
The boyfriend
was part of her cover
the elaborate impersonation
of an American teenager
almost everyone engaged in
a vast communal experiment

which led
for white people to consequences
& sociological reflection & TV series
She couldn't see
the boyfriend she could sense
him sort of
nothing clear
She was too much
in her own way
not to mention the boyfriend's
and the crazed mirror
of her self-absorption
intervened a veritable Versailles
of ostentatious non-encounter
in plexiglassed and lockered halls
He was a good
enough boyfriend
for a while
&/so in an experimental
spirit one day
she sd I love you
She didn't
and she didn't
quite not.
It was a thing
to try
out the fatal
banal words
a paradigm
shift so they sd

Nothing
shifted but the deep
tectonic plates that constitute the crust
of her
core shifted
in a spasm
of self-disgust
She didn't feel
it & she didn't not
Why say anything
I heard words
and words full
of holes
aching
Words
are deeds
True and False
Truth or Dare
her tongue
her self
a forked
unknowing thing
that sang two parts
unharmonizing
Even then she saw
the decent boy
with a queer
remoteness
He wasn't up
for her project

of violent self
formation
& soon faded
into the unfinished basement
of her mind

Mz N No Permanent Mind

The great thing
is not having
a mind Mz N read
many years after
she'd acquired
a somewhat permanent
mind. She had a theory
about this situation
inchoate for some years
but which she called in retrospect
and retroactively
"No permanent mind
condition" which was
her condition
How could anyone think
they persisted
in time
& over?
How did anyone know
anything they knew
would be what they knew
tomorrow?
These
were the imponderables
she pondered or was brought to

by "experience"
a noun she didn't believe in
Was this condition
brought on by a crack
in the mind-
brain continuum?
Was it a function
of inadequate parenting some undone
mirroring somehow the world breeding
a lack of faith
in the ongoingness
of self & world?
Was it
she was too sensitive
as the chorus insisted
This is not the same thing
This was a mental
thing with emotional
implications. Since she was a stranger
to herself at any moment
everything it seemed passed
right through her nothing stayed
there was no there
there in the there
of her mind
For
example
she changed schools
several times in crucial years
the pre- and teen

years when the carnival
of thinking and feeling
one's way into whatever
was in full swing.
She knew nothing
most especially the things
she once knew. Each time
she ventured
into a new classroom she greeted
the new world
naked, stripped
of certainty the Tilt-a-Whirl unhinged
from its frame
the lurid requirement
of socialization and piano lessons
facing her a sicko clownface
HAHAHAHAHA FUCK YOU
Everyone tells stories
of how they became X or Y thing
identity identity
what was identity
it seemed a fragile thing
to be
& brittle the chains
identity
She could not escape
the predicament
of being one
among other ones but sometimes
it could be sung

into an elsewhere of co-being
This was chorus
The chorus
comments on the action
& sometimes partakes.
Chorus
presupposes a chosen submission
to the fusion
of co-created sound
Out of many one
or many as the case may be
It would have been useful
if the chorus were Greek and they'd been consulted
or at least asked to respond
to the actions
of the main actors.
Who were the main actors?
Most people
feel themselves
to be some kind of actor even Mrs. Ramsay
though she acts
more as a stage manager
invisible-handing the courtships along
and soothing the Mister
is an actor
Her knitting is a deep action
Children
are so often the chorus
in life
but not much heard

as they are not yet of the citizenry
Mz N had a horror
of most groups
though she joined several
which came from a horror of the pressure
of coercion countered by the pressure
of having to think about everything
from the ground up she felt continuously
the iron logic
of what was obvious
yet so perilous
everyone furiously strained
to keep it so
Viz. God
Viz. Family
Viz. Good behavior
Mz N lacked the courage
to smoke
herself out of her covert she tried
to read Nietzsche
but failed what was he saying What
what was he What was he saying
She felt he would answer
to something failed
& instead of reading lived out
the death of god
in her life

The major genres
of modernity are not interested

in this story
& Mz N is often uninterested
isn't this interesting
how the bourgeois individual
was always making himself
against a horizon of love
& work which resolved into
his own projection of a classed grid
a kind of massive erection of the self
amidst the machinery
of institutions—
Well
There are other nodes
Other genres
Other genders
One can be visible
in the world & invisible
One can be a glacier
only the tip of yourself visible
in the open cold blue air

Mz N Hater

Mz N wants to be like Hazlitt
a great hater
There is so much
to hate   The haters
The mingy minions
of the lesser courts
who attend the chatterati
The fetid fawners
The kissup/kickdown
crapola crew
The given arrangements
called "the world"
But most and first her self
      shame/contempt
      shame/contempt
      systole/diastole of a faulty pump
      i.e. Mz N
If she were true
to "herself"
she would be a hermit
turn isolato
take the narrow road
to the deep North
with Bashō and his tired horse
leave deathless lines

at every bamboo'd stop
catch the words
of whores and kids en route
& the lonely sound of rain
O to take the path
of a hundred weathered bones
and nine orifices
to take a pseudonym
under a banana tree
to travel true
anonymous as a variable
under the sign
of an adopted tree
one carries invisible on a bent back
A windswept spirit finally open
to whatever

Mz N Thirteenth Floor

Let's say he lives
on the 13th floor
which exists despite superstition
and the hookers hang
in the foyer mingling
with the more or less
respectable not that they
don't of course deserve etcetera
An apartment by the lake
If this were the '50s
it would be a pad
a bachelor pad all Frank
and martinis and swank
It has that vibe
though it's not the '50s
and he's not Ol' Blue Eyes
though he has blue eyes
He's an explorer
of sensation ethnographer
videographer of the real
He is muy curioso
and concedes a tendency
toward nostalgia
regarding other lives
he might have lived   What ho

In this one life
to live stay tuned
at 11 he's directing
an episode starring
though she doesn't know it
Mz N who seems up
more or less for anything
though maybe it's just
she's apathetic
So hard to distinguish
the oh sure from whatever
She doesn't talk
He doesn't ask
It seems intrusive
Language a late
mammalian acquisition
Why not stick
to the gestural now
He is nothing
if not not intrusive
He's debonair his savoir faire
a thing raw
Americans lack.
He has a reputation
as an excellent lover
conveyed by an ex-lover
a potential lover of Mz N
O roundelay
O lurch & sway
& dip & swing

He's adept at partnering
with a mellow almost joie
de vivre if joie were leavened
by a sharp observing
and self-remembering
In his silent way
he's observing
how she'll accept
this latest role in the latest play
Location: his bedroom
Prop: saran wrap
Prop: duct tape
Prop: bed
Direction: wrap him
Blocking: he tells her
to stand there & wrap him
Wrap him head to toe
He is in his bedroom
naked he commands her
wrap him
head to toe
& then implicitly
fuck him
& bemused she obeys
Well what is this
Well who could say
One supposes it heightens
sensation O strap O leather
O rubber O latex of dungeon
masks of the focalized

sensorium now
O deprivation
you rev my motorcar
you take me oh you take me oh so far
Is that Pat Metheny
on the turntable
was that a bottle
of wellchosen red
did it make
for an interesting
night? She follows through
but he can't help
thinking her
a disappointment
Why can't she embrace
the occasion initiate
an action   Everything
he has to do everything
just like the guy
who wanted to fuck Mz N
's friend up the ass
but she was eh
she was not so into it not least
because she wasn't into him
so why give up her ass
even out of curiosity
Why is everything a giving
up a giving up your X or Y
I'd be promiscuous
if I weren't so contemptuous

this friend told Mz N one night
Uh huh
Everybody
has a thing
they really want
and no one will give it to them
& that's the thing they want
Desire
is endless
disappointment
Desire is lack
blah blah blah
Is this true is it
an endlessly renewed
box of crayons
all gone gray
The gray scale
of her sensuality
is dampening his jouissance recipe
the coño bomb he wants to set off
between her breasts defused
smooth jazz all the way

Mz N Therapy

Mz N has a friend
who is who's dying
Hello friend
Don't die
Don't prove
yet again
the omnipotence of thoughts
a lie
I command you
live! Thus Mz N commanded
her friend
who is now dead
She was
in the first instance
to Mz N
a voice
on the phone and after
that interview and another
in person
her therapist
Mz N was a case
of extremity
thus therapy
enabled by health insurance
and a state

of emergency
and Illinois and a university
Sometimes Mz N loves
the state
wants to pay more taxes
pledge allegiance fill out a census every day
then lapses her whole life
a lapse & no felix
culpa why was she
all to-torne
as in Chaucer
why was she
so friendly
with her local abyss
that to her was global
Well
There are things
one could say about that
and the therapist did
but mainly let Mz N spool out
what she needed to
the enormous coil the tangled innards
One could spin the thread
into any number of fabrics
designs or fates or snip them
Mz N had never gone
to therapy
it wasn't in the family
repertoire and somewhere
deep within she knew

if she went she'd shatter
She was shattered
so she went
all the billion shards
of her held in a cup
in Chicago by the lake
a great blue lake
that seemed the unblinking eye
of a cold alien god
There was nothing
not worth talking about
not worth being quiet about
How interesting silences
How interesting the little rages
upsurging
for years
this woman
who was mainly a voice
a tall presence
with stupendous breasts foregrounded
surely by whatever stage
of regression Mz N was then in
This is such an old hermeneutic
it stinks of the '90s
the 1890s and cocaine and hysteria
& fin-de-siècle inquiry
and that is where she had to be
in the late 20th century
Mz N was always belated
to herself

as one is
It is so hard
to be contemporary
especially with oneself
always living forward thinking
backward Hello
Present Tense
Because she was paying
to have a dreamlife she had one
filled with terrors and clichés
& she wrote them her dreams down
acquiring a stunning facility
in waking recall
or was it invention
O doubt
O neurosis
Those days
Mz N was closer
to psychosis
stayed clear
perhaps stupidly
of the brainsoothing drugs
which would
her friends told her
put a floor under her
She wasn't walking
She was flying
a grinning demon
in Bosch a lurid hell
of florid-colored pains

My mind to me
a torment is
I am *both a burden and a terror*
to myself
she sd and dreamed
her first official therapy dream
featuring Gertrude Stein
& a cigar which struck her
as rather obvious
There was no way to think
about everything feel it all
out from the ground of being
up. Sometimes
you just have to go
with it
She was
she admitted
stuck
stuck in a crashed plane
she dreamed her friend
might open a door
from   O would she   would she
She awoke
The therapist was patient
glamorous engaging
& yet not usually
intrusive
which was a plus
People are stupid
and mediocre

years later she sd
reflecting on the human condition
brought home to her by her death sentence
It is still possible
for genius
to go unrecognized
in America
Mz N knows it
she knows her friend a genius
who's dead.
What is a genius
A genius channels the spirit
of original
creation singularly
Or, *To believe*
your own thought, to believe
that what is true for you
in your private heart is true
for all—
that is genius
A genius
usually has to make something
and if you just are
if you just privately exist
then you can go missing
as a genius
Talents untried
are talents unknown.
I should have shown myself
more in the world

she said
then died
What is waste
What is loss
Therapy
was the worst experience
of Mz N's life
except for those experiences
which brought her to therapy.
It was arduous
an ordeal a test a trial
agon acid bath
of introspection
& co-feeling barely held
together in the cup of the room
Strange soul technē
peculiar praxis the Vale
of Soul-Making had come
to this O Thel
running from the Vale of Har
stay put stay where you are—

Fare forward woman
wherever the eternal are

Mz N Baby

One day her sister
asked Mz N
to have her baby
This was intriguing
this was frightening
as there had been no babies
come thru her
& to have a baby
not her baby
seemed a strong hard thing
to split the body for.
Shitting
a pumpkin
is what a friend
of Shulamith Firestone
said in the late '60s
it was like
This birth thing
This birthing
The midwives
were gathering
a sharp-eyed coven prepared
to elbow out
the doctors who after all
have long done harm

as much as not.
Mz N's sister
didn't quite ask her
It was more a raising
of the question.
All that summer
she thought
along a country road
about this thing.
Not to the future
but the fuchsia
she thought eyeing
the dicentra and misremembering
Gertrude Stein.
Not the past
but the last possible thing
Isn't it strange to think
I have a dick
in me the pregnant teen said
to her dismayed dad
in a short story.
More stories
these days embrace babies.
Before
they were there
more as ghost cries.
There he goes crowing
sd Gertrude Stein
of Hemingway
about the birth of his son

as if a million men
every day
weren't fathers.
She had a point
but still.
That little baby
is Bumby
in *A Moveable Feast*.
There was nothing
more romantic
than the way
Hem and his wife
shared a bottle of wine
in their bare cabin
in the winter woods
I used to think.
The whole book
seemed a valentine
from another time.
He sd they were poor
& repeated it
but I didn't believe it.
That baby grew up
& did not kill himself
unlike his father and grandfather.
Babies
are romantic
if they are subordinate.
The minute
they rise up all scream

it's a new wound.
Why not let yourself
be torn?
Why not let anything
be born?
Mz N wondered
how anyone
ever made a decision
especially women.
Reason
is but choosing
but there are so many reasons.
Choice
is a fallacy
sustained by the ideology
of the individual
says a friend of Mz N.
Nevertheless.
The thrush
doesn't choose to sing
but sings
& the maple
can't choose not to leaf out
& Mz N can't choose
not to drift
through a summer of possibles
& unresolved doubts

Mz N Woman

One day Mz N meets a woman
slightly horsefaced
hair a tangle
strong teeth and features
eyes black pools
Who knew this
was beauty
Not Mz N
Not yet
Eros is a hard god
Eros is sly
It is always the case
Mz N never feels the arrow
right away
It takes days
months years then
where that arrow hit
BANG O Now
O Now Mz N Doth Feel It
So hard to align
the when & then
Jetztzeit of the stricken moment
for she was eternal stricken
knew it
by a dream

when making love with X
she woke and
O
not this not O
& there
unavoidable now
the new mouth
she'd move through
this new thing
new tongue new lungs
suckerpunched sucker
dread delight
O Sappho what do you want this time
A revelation can be violent
the tearing the rending
of the veil aletheia
the truth of the soul
lurching for what it wants
cunt a pulse
and most the tube
of the chest blown through
the body all instrument
for this new breathing

Mz N Moon

There is a long debate
among the philosophers
of love do you love
the beloved or her qualities
It's clear Mz N loves
the beloved asleep
right now in the swart tent
they set out in the night
in the moon's slow rising
in love's remembering
With how sad steps
the moon has climbed
the skies & with glad steps
it now arises mounts
the sky and hangs above
an old mountain.
If the owl and the pussycat
went to sea in a beautiful
pea-green boat & if love
quotes Edward Lear
she is more dear
but not the beloved
for that. The Elizabethans
got it wrong
with their endlessly inventive

and reiterative blazons
itemizing love as if
love were a rhetorical series
contained in a little song
and not the thrust push
& lull of song going
on and on and on
as if love's plum lips
hips and breasts
long thighs and singularly arched
brows lakeblue eyes
the golden zone the swell
and all & praised
could ever begin to raise
the sail on the boat
now setting forth
on a moonlit pond

Mz N Palinode

Just like you
to sing a flower song
of love   ignore
the lash of labor
you're not under

Just like you
to lean on a lyre
float in a meadow
when the cracking world
needs action, facts

Just like you
to set a course
then lose yourself
in Siren's siren

your little privacies
now whirling
down the pool
of something else required

Did you not think
the world larger

Are the old songs
all wrong

In her next life
Mz N will be serious
and public and save
the republic
turn singularity
into solidarity
or retreat
into a silence
proper to a chaos
that eludes any kiss
or word of a kiss

SOME SAY

OK Let's Go

Let's go to Dawn School
and learn again to begin

oh something different
from repetition

Let's go to the morning
and watch the sun smudge

every bankrupt idea
of nature "you can't write about

anymore" said my friend
the photographer "except

as science"
Let's enroll ourselves

in the school of the sky
where knowing

how to know
and unknow is everything

we'll come to know
under what they once thought

was the dome of the world

Mesh

Everything in the world
has a name
if you know it.
You know that.

The fungus
secreting itself
from the bark
is Colt's Hoof.

The dignity
of cataloguers
bows before code.

The thing
about elements—
they don't want
to be split

Every time
I collide with your mind
I give off—
something happens—
we don't know what

Particles, articles
this bit, a bit
digital, simple
fission, fusion
—a great vowel shift.

I saw the world
dissolve in waves
the trees as one
with the sun
and their shadows.

The trees on the shore
The trees in the pond
branch in the mind

The screech of the subway
decelerating its knife
into the brain
of all riders

In the morning the hummingbird
In the evening five deer

Why should I feel bad
about beauty?

The postmodernists
are all rational
& sad though they mug

in zany gear.
Everyone knows
what is happening
They disagree why
& what then.

It turns out
the world was made for us
to mesh.

Some Say

Some say a host
of horsemen, a horizon
of ships under sail
is most beautiful &
some say a mountain
embraced by the clouds &
some say the badass
booty-shakin' shorties
in the club are most
beautiful and some say
the truth is most
beautiful dutifully singing
what beauty might
sound under stars
of a day. I say
what they say
is sometimes
what I say
Her legs long
and bare shining
on the bed the hair
the small tuft
the brown languor
of a long line
of sunlit skin I say

whatever you say
I'm saying is beautiful
& whither truth beauty
and whither whither
in the weather of an old day
suckerpunched by a spiral
of Arctic air blown
into vast florets of ice
binding the Great Lakes
into a single cracked sheet
the airplanes fly
unassuming over   O they eat
and eat the steel mouths
and burn what the earth
spun eons to form
Some say calamity
and some catastrophe
is beautiful   Some say
porn   Some jolie laide
Some say beauty
is hanging there at a dank bar
with pretty and sublime
those sad bitches left behind
by the horsemen

Forest

There you go
walking in the woods
as usual
ignoring the trees . . .

The fifteen kinds
of trees
you refuse
to lodge in your skull.

Here's the stand
of Norway spruce
mostly dead.
Someone's bad idea.

We are going
to monetize
everything
so value shines
clear as the sun.

Just because,
things happen

Just because
things happened
doesn't absolve
whoever's alive

The future's
a lure
& hungry fish bite.
Curious.

You want
a solid Lutheran hymn
to praise the given
under the sign of salvation.

God an organ
few now know
how to play.

Diapason,
Aeoline Celeste—
So many stops
to make the sound
of what used to be
the greatest machine

He knew all the names
and if he appeared

to the forest people
he appeared as a rainbow bird
on the supreme tree

There you go
making images
because you don't know the names.

Taking a Walk in the Woods After Having Taken a Walk in the Woods with You

Now I cannot not see
the blight everywhere

The relativity

of pests:
how I felt
about you
fifty minutes into
a call that while
not deeply annoying
was truly boring
The deer that first appeared
a dark mass
against a distant tree
resolved into a beauty
of dun fawn
the long-tuned elegance
of an ancient body
now riddled with ticks
O there are too many
& we must cull
we will shoot humanely
what's excessively
about to wipe
us or our friends
out but let's wait
on killing
sentiment

gets its moment
here before the gun
the archaic click
of a phone back on the hook

Prospect

Thus should have been our life
sexual, untaxable . . .
And the tyranny of thumbs
and hips and skulls
which brought us down from the trees
and condemned us to permanent screens
was a regime no declaration
could free us from.
You are too young
to think so much
about death she sd
the older woman
who dressed in her
long-trained dancer's muscles
did not seem old
as we are made to see them
residual forgettable a little shameful
but one must not hurt them lest
the fragile carapace under which
we live ramshackled days
shatter, as if in a thought experiment
of a world without oxygen for five seconds
become a world in free fall
all untreated metals
spontaneously welding together

& our every cell exploding
in a hydrogen collapse.
Melancholia is realism
and realisms are isms and
the thing itself retreats
into the forest now there &
there calling the first new bird
in spring unheard
for four long months
What was a month to the men
with only a moon & a sun

*

Once upon a time
when everyone had pubic hair
and read books and had been taught
penmanship and bombs
and oh good PB&J there was pleasure
in things specifically now
forgotten or rather abandoned
Let's forsake the crusted nostalgia
of the global ruling classes
Go fist yourself
a roasted duck on a warm spit

*

Let us be decorative and unafraid
Let us approach the line at the edge of a margin of a bay

& love the asymptotic whatever
Let us salute the clouds even when they shit on us
as if the earth were an excrement of some sky
and we still saluted it
Let all the centuries collapse
into endless columns of clouds
we the survivors look on

Peony

There's a woman
walks through me
sits at the table
reading Rumi
You are in your body
as a plant is in the earth
yet you are yes the wind
and she is bending
into the wind her death
and she is a thin tree
and what she never saw
this peony

White Dress

It is not too late to wear a white dress my love though the fall
suspends itself in the trees
whose leaves shine a green wind that will not pass
until it passes this day the boat you pick up and lift
off the pond it too ripples
& the duck skitters to a landing
all the world a sudden field
to land in   Why dive
when one can glide in a white dress
well-groomed feathers the ruffled pond
will fit in your pocketbook
your pocketbook will fit
in the knapsack where all the tools
of the visible are labeled
and ready—we know how to fix everything
today, the sky its cirrus and the grass
browning without rain without
rain nothing grows but the mind
its bones unbending

It is not too late to wear your sandals love though we live
far from the desert the desert is here its sands in the soles
of your sandals the desert is the shifting plain
we've not yet visited and the Tuareg
have yet to climb the White Mountains

It is not too late love to know everyone
& everything shines a weird light the pantheists
call soul the fortunetellers aura or something
the realists scoff at oh the sad scoffers and mickey mockers
Is it too late to buy them a drink

Is it too late to wear a delicate necklace
fashioned by a Greek artist you've never met
Too late to say hey what was all that fuss
about the asteroid Too late to buy the burial plot
And is it too early to say some days it seems just Wow
you look so elegant there unadorned in a white dress
& sandals at the perfect juncture of the season
and life oh do not bend your head any further lest the stalk break
the flower of the now

For You

It's been a long while since I was up before you
but here I am, up before you.

I see you sleeping now that I am up before you.
I see the whole morning before you.

How dare the sun be up before you
when the moon last night promised to hold off the sun just for you!

I hear the church bells ring before you.
Most days it's true the birds are up before you.

I should make the coffee, as I am up before you.
I might just lie here though before you

wake up. Let me look at you, since I am here before you.
I am so rarely simply quiet before you.

The orange cat who'll soon wake you is always up before you.
In Morocco or Lamu the muezzin would be up before you.

And yes it's true most days the sun is up before you—
long before me and a while before you.

Shall I make it a habit to be up before you?
To see your soft cheek and feel your breath if I am up before you?

Shall I prepare the mise-en-scène for you?
Hold the shot of the sun in my eye just for you?

Go back to sleep my love for you
are only dreaming I am up before you.

Crux / Fern Park

In the otherwise untroubled snow
I saw where I'd turned around

faint gashes the trace in the snow
of the way my mind ran aground

on the question of which way to go
There was no way to know the direction

from a thinning sun
no way to follow the hum

of snowmobiles to a possible road
The way I stood was pressed in the snow

the first ski marks almost effaced
by a second and then a third guess

distressing the snow with poles
and the old lust to move

even at 5° below
and only a chickadee

and a black unidentifiable thing
out of the corner of the eye

running through the woods
clearly knew their own going

No roads diverged
no ski trail split

the mind forked itself
and doubled back

and back and back
among the black spruce and tamaracks

One Canoe

Recalcitrant elephants
begin to attack.
The angry young males
of murdered mothers

Any Martian could see it
how we did it

The historian of the future
is amazed. So much feeling

once in so many bodies.
*But maybe they were different
didn't think or feel that much.*

Apocalypse is easy
Thinking's hard

Should we summon
a Roman Stoic to narrate?
Someone secretly thrilled
by the gore?

The clouds move through
an Adirondack sky unscored
by satellite towers.

People want what they want
& what they want is never one thing.

All that desire
sliming a space rock.

Shivering the air
a loon's cry.
There is only so much
you can care for or carry

& for this there is
no one canoe

Girls in Bed

You are in bed
and Antigone's dead

once again though offstage
and alive on the previous page

doomed proud girl
elective fatalist

& the dark Doñas
and perved-out girls

are facing off
at the Met

Velázquez
vs. Balthus

and you know who
wins. A sleeping

woman is an erotic
thing in many a painting

and Albertine sleeps
away it seems

a million days
as Proust swerves

ever unto a swerving
desire. But/And

you are sleeping
and no one's painting

or writing or looking
You're sleeping by the cat

in another room
and Sinatra croons a tune

"as charming as hell even yet"
on NPR. Where we are

isn't fixed by any GPS
or pinpointed location

can't be mapped by street name
city state or nation

O the drift as between
America and Europe

as between girls
in bed and girls dead

The vast Atlantic
suddenly reveals

itself a thin
watery thing covering

a continental shelf
An Atlantean upsurge

cracks the abyssal plain
proves what looks sundered

is so deep under linked

On Not Being Elizabethan

How did they do it
shape their complex minds
into chiming lines
of woe & sorrow
crowning frowning
every rhyme sieved in time
to a bell they all heard ringing
Singing no more singing
but stinging an enemy
into his own dole and song
decrying everything
the enemy said
as the enemy's wrong
When the mind's a ready surface
the stamp's impress will take
What is it to suffer
the mood of a queen
It seems ridiculous
a sudden kiss
a glance or gesture
a vow a letter
derailing a life
unto a dungeon tower
An insurrection every hour
it seems I suffer

Can she excuse my wrongs
with virtue's cloak?
Can I compose this song
of air and ancient smoke?
The fires still burn
Dead hearts still yearn
A tiny repertoire
of end rhymes enough
to win a queen an empire
enough to set a cold heart afire
enough to make an English lute
a Greek lyre
enough to make the killing block
a singing pyre

Headphones

The French Revolution vanishes
into rain.

The café where Camille Desmoulins
jumped atop the table and roared
is closed.

So too the one grocery store
in the Adirondack town.

Three years fade
into centuries of raised voices.

When I think "of my childhood"
what am I thinking?

Spiro Agnew's widow died.
Everything a function
of stochastic patterns
this rain also obeys.

Can't you hear it
the unpitched wave soaking
the spruce?

Can't you hear them screaming?
Morton Feldman said
pointing below the Berlin pavement stones.

One deafens to live
till you're deafened to all.

I'm canceling all the noise
my earthened ears bring me.

Against the
Promise of a View

A difficult climb
to a beautiful view—
I don't like it.
I don't like the way
you make me go
positively Protestant
all this deferral
up to a future
only you've seen
the ascent always leveraged
against an alien payoff
already prescripted.
When we get there
I'll be dead
tired too tired to view
the view the way
I wanted. I wanted
the way to be beautiful
as a stroll in the Hanging
Gardens of Babylon
or the wisteria-laden
lanes of the rose garden
in the Bois de Boulogne
as beautiful as a jammed

Sixth Avenue crosswalk
in midtown. I wanted
to be going nowhere
nowhere we know
not to have to breathe
so hard into a future
someone else promised.
I know
reputable studies show
the capacity
to delay
gratification
makes for a happy
person & nation
but oh
I just want
& want now
a perpetual
beautiful stroll
nowhere
I don't want
to look back
& say ah
that was so
worth it
because even
if it was
it wasn't.
I don't want
to keep my head down
for miles alert

for insurgent roots
a falling branch
my legs punctured
by stinging flies
that harry the way
only to be able to say
at some notional
top however beautiful
how beautiful
—& see, no insects here
& why not lunch—
Somehow
it was just
the glorious sun
and twelve islands
inlaid in a lake
& the distant silent
powerboats
Somehow it was a vision
of all as dust
If I go
on pilgrimage
I want every age
to be a stage
one can look around
and say how interesting
& yes a cup of coffee
would be nice
I'm not going anywhere
fast but where
we're all going

Night Sky

Spackled black
the pure uncertain light
invites you to climb
a ladder on a clear night
to a vanished point

Messages arriving
the messengers long dead
& the airplanes traversing the stars
in their flight are carrying
the future dead

Metal wombs
for earthly angels
sleeping in rationed seats
The trays don't easily fold back up
now that dinner service is complete

The baggage is checked
stored above and below
The attendants provide
blanket and pillow

All day and night the sky alive
with wanderers

who nonetheless know
where they are going
because the ticket says so

and in a long look
a still point moves slow
across a climacteric
you hadn't thought to trace
or to that satellite
to give a specific national face

The man in the moon
is the hare making rice cakes
in Japan & the stars long ago
swallowed the Greeks

They look back at us dumb
in their old religion
The belt of Orion encircles
no man's hips
and Cassandra is crying out
through foregone lips

A crab crawls and fish swim
in unscannable seas
The sky drinks
in its black miseries

A comfort to sailors
who take two seamarks

One mark will never suffice
in the unmarked dark

When an unseen hand
or death metal band
crumples the sky
in untellable folds

see the North Star kiss Mars
& Venus unveil her face
as admen brand the stars
and men sell shares in space
the multiverse contracts
to a single implacable place
where nothing you can imagine
will never not take place

Acknowledgments

The poems in this collection were originally published in the following:

This Carrying Life (Boston: Arrowsmith, 2005)
This Carrying Life II (Boston: Arrowsmith/Pressed Wafer, 2006)
Same Life (New York: Farrar, Straus and Giroux, 2008)
World Enough (New York: Farrar, Straus and Giroux, 2010)
This Blue (New York: Farrar, Straus and Giroux, 2014)
Mz N: the serial (New York: Farrar, Straus and Giroux, 2016)
Some Say (New York: Farrar, Straus and Giroux, 2017)

Several poems in this book first appeared in a Pressed Wafer broadside of April 2005. "One Canoe" appeared in a feuilleton, *Parallels*, edited by Alice Lyons, Curator, Poetry Now, 2015, for the Mountains to Sea dlr Book Festival in Dún Laoghaire, Ireland. "Night Sky" was first published in a chapbook, *New Year* (edited by Will Vincent, 2014), accompanying the screening of Adam Shecter's video *New Year* (2014) at 11R Gallery, New York City. The last poem in "Core Samples" was the basis for Sam Sadigursky's composition "Ode," on his album "Words Project III Miniatures" (2010). "For You" has been set to music by the composer Judah Adashi. It was first performed by Caroline Shaw (voice) and Caleb Burhans (viola) in 2016. All thanks to these artists, poets, musicians, and editors.

I am grateful to the editors, publishers, and staffs of the following journals, in which some of these poems first appeared, sometimes in slightly different form: The Academy of American Poets "Poem-A-Day" Series, *American Letters & Commentary, The American Reader, American Scholar, Blackbox Manifold, The Canary, Circumference: poetry in translation, The Cortland Review, Eborakon, Granta, GREY, Harvard Review, Jacket, jubilat,* the *Kenyon Review, Literary Hub, Literary Imagination, London Review of Books, The Nation, The New Republic, The New Yorker, nonsite.org, Painted, Spoken, The Paris Review, Plume, Poetry, Poetry Daily, Port, Prac Crit, Psychology Tomorrow, A Public Space, Shearsman Magazine, Slate, The Spectator, Tin House, T: The New York Times Style Magazine,* and *The Wallace Stevens Journal.*

For their care with and generous attention to this book, thanks to Jeff Clark, Logan Hill, and Katie Liptak.

For support during the writing of these poems, deepest thanks to Blue Mountain Center, the Hedgebrook Foundation, the Liguria Study Center for the Arts and Humanities/the Bogliasco Foundation, MacDowell, the Columbia Institute for Scholars (Reid Hall, Paris), the New York University Global Research Initiative, Santa Maddalena Foundation, and Yaddo. I am grateful to these institutions and the provisional communities and enduring friendships they sponsored.

And to those who asked or answered: Rachael Allen, David Baker, Ed Barrett, Sara Bershtel, Frank Bidart, Diane Boller, Matthew Campbell, David Caplan, Eric William Carroll, Rob Casper, John Clegg, Beverly Corbett, the late William Corbett, Kelvin Corcoran, Valerie Cotter, Robyn Creswell, Alex Dimitrov, Jeff Dolven, Bart Eeckhout, Ellen Eisenman, Adam Fitzgerald, Dai George, Eileen Gillooly, Lisa Goldfarb, Saskia Hamilton, Langdon Hammer, Hugh Haughton, Stefania Heim, Cathy Park Hong, Alex Houen, Sarah Howe, Valentina Ilardi, Oren Izenberg, Bill Jacobson, Amy Johnson, Devin Johnston, Paul Keegan, August Kleinzahler, Cheston Knapp, Jennifer Kronovet, Danny Lawless, Brantly Martin, Askold Melnyczuk, Erica Mena, Ange Mlinko, Diana Morse, Paul Muldoon, Matt Neff, Luke Neima, Karl O'Hanlon, Meghan O'Rourke, Tony Perez, Adam Piette, Richard Price, Alice Quinn, Justin Quinn, Vidyan Ravinthiran, Catherine Robson, Alane Rollings, Don Selby, Don Share, Dinos Siotis, Ersi Sotiropoulos, Lorin Stein, Jack Thacker, JT Welsch, Clair Wills, and especially, first and last, all thanks to Jonathan Galassi.

A grateful salute as well to Antoine Compagnon, Emily Drury, the late Barbara Ess, Anne-Lise François, Dylan Gauthier, Louise Glück, Bruce King, Celeste Langan, Timothy Morton, Anahid Nersessian, Victoria Olwell, Katie Peterson, Tom Pickard, Kirstin Valdez Quade, Yvonne Rainer, Karen Russell, Tino Sehgal, Shelly Silver, Carole Slatkin, Ben Strader, and Kendra Sullivan: whose thoughts, work, and comments diversely vibrate here.

In memoriam Shahab Ahmed; Richard Brick; William Corbett; Patrizia Lombardo; Julia Targ.

For my teachers, dead and alive, human and not.

For my parents, and for my siblings, their partners and children . . . family given and chosen.

With and for whom: Laura—so much more, anon . . .

Index of Titles and First Lines

envoi: eclipse

I don't trust myself
not to look